I0177415

DIVINE KEYS TO UNLOCKING YOUR DESTINY

A 30-DAY JOURNEY TO UNLOCKING YOUR DESTINY

CHERYL DYSON-BENNETT

Divine Keys to Unlocking Your Destiny
© 2021 Cheryl Dyson-Bennett

All rights reserved. This book is printed in the United States of America. No part of this book may be used or reproduced in any form or by any means -electronic, mechanical, photocopy, recording, or otherwise - without written permission of the publisher, except in the case of brief quotations embodied in critical articles or reviews.

THE HOLY BIBLE, NEW INTERNATIONAL VERSION, NIV Copyright© 1973, 1978, 1984, 2011, by Biblica, Inc. Used by permission. All rights reserved worldwide.

Scriptures taken from the New King James Version. Copyright© 1982 by Thomas Nelson. Used by permission. All rights reserved.

Scripture quotations marked KJV are from the King James Version of the Bible.

Scripture quotations marked NLT are from the Holy Bible, New Living Translation, Copyright© 1996, 2004, 2007. Used by permission. All rights reserved.

Scripture quotations marked The Message are from The Message: The Bible in Contemporary English, Copyright© 1993, 1994, 1995, 2000, 2001, 2002. Used by permission. All rights reserved.

Designed for Greatness
Atlanta, Georgia
www.designed4greatness.com

You are Designed for Greatness; I am Designed for Greatness; We are Designed for Greatness.

Table of Contents

INTRODUCTION

Destiny is a beautiful gift that God keeps in us; it is our purpose, and our assignment. It is the sum of who we are and are capable of becoming. Also, destiny is the potential we have, our journey towards realizing them, and the achievements that must count as stars being added to our crowns.

Contrary to popular opinion, your destiny is not just about your destination; it is about your whole journey on earth. Your destiny is more of a journey. The journey to the end of your life should be taken as the essence of living. What makes up the gospel of Christ is the birth, life, death, and resurrection of Jesus; not just that He died to become the captain of our salvation.

It is good that you look forward to becoming who you want to be, but it is even better that you enjoy the whole transformational process that God is taking you through. This is because every point matter: from birth to childhood, and from childhood to adulthood. Since destiny encapsulates the totality of man, why do people only focus on the endpoint?

Unlocking your destiny is not an event; it is a journey. You need to understand that everyday matters. The key you find today can unlock the door where the next key is. There is no master key when it comes to destiny; there are unique keys that would give different individuals access to their destinies. The same key might not work for everyone, because we are different, and our needs are different.

This devotional is a book and a journey; a key, as it houses several keys that you will need on your journey. As you read, study, and meditate on these pages, may you find rest for your soul, understanding to your mind, and light to your path.

There are key applications for you to put into your action plan, so you can take practical steps toward adopting the key. Likewise, there are key prayer points that will guide you on what and how to pray.

Are you ready for the outcome of the unlocking?

KEY 1
GRACE

> "And He said to me, "My grace is sufficient for you, for My strength is made perfect in weakness." Therefore most gladly I will rather boast in my infirmities, that the power of Christ may rest upon me." (2 Corinthians 12:9 NKJV)

Grace is favor. It is the free and undeserved help that God gives us to respond to His call to become His children, adoptive sons, partakers of the divine nature, and of eternal life. It is the unmerited divine assistance given to humans for their regeneration or sanctification. By the simplest definition, grace is simply "unmerited favor" or "unconditional love." It is a virtue, approval, or favor that comes from God.

> "And of His fullness we have all received, and grace for grace. For the law was given through Moses, but grace and truth came through Jesus Christ." (John 1:16-17 NKJV)

The grace of God came to us through Jesus Christ. While on the cross, He took all the punishment that we deserved and placed it on Himself. Also, He gave us the gift of a relationship with God; something we do not deserve or earn by ourselves. God demonstrated His love to us, His children, by giving Christ to us. Meanwhile, grace does not stop once we are saved; God is gracious to us for the rest of our lives, as He works within and upon us, in all that we do.

> *"For it is by grace you have been saved, through faith—and this is not from yourselves, it is the gift of God—not by works, so that no one can boast. For we are God's handiwork, created in Christ Jesus to do good works, which God prepared in advance for us to do"* (Ephesians 2:8-10).

One aspect of salvation we will focus on is called justification. It is the act by which we are declared just (righteous) before God based on the payment Jesus Christ made for our sins. We are told that we have been saved "by grace" but "through faith" in God. Grace is seen here as the means by which we are saved. As a gift, faith is seen as the mechanism by which salvation or grace is appropriated.

The grace of God is not limited to the gift of salvation; it offers us much more, especially, all that pertains to life and godliness, so we might live and lead successful lives in all we do. In Titus 2:11-12, grace brought salvation, and this grace also teaches us how to live in this present age.

The grace of God can teach us things that people might not understand, which can give us an advantage towards fulfilling our destinies. The grace of God can help you unlock your destiny in Christ and in life. The grace of God selects and separates you from others (Romans 11:5). When grace comes upon anointing, gift, or wealth, it multiplies (Genesis 33:8-11). Grace empowers you to witness Christ in your unique area of calling, which could be your career, business, or even ministry.

We can receive grace upon grace by approaching God's throne (Hebrews 4:16). From this same scripture, we will realize that grace helps us in our every need. Also, grace is the reason behind our every deliverance. Grace provides us access to God to communicate and fellowship with Him. As recipients of God's grace, Christians are to be gracious to others. Grace is given to us to serve others and exercise our spiritual gifts to buildup the church.

Key Application

1. Live in the fullness of all that the death of Jesus purchased for you.

2. Understand God's destiny for your life, and know that His promises to you, cannot be

hindered by your current situation. As you grow in the intimate knowledge of Jesus, His grace and peace will continually multiply in your life.

3. Be assured that as you delve into the Holy Scriptures, your youth and mind will be renewed, and you will become aware of all the vast treasury of the great and precious promises that have been granted to you.

4. Turn your back on the world that has already turned its back on you.

Key Prayer

1. Lord, help me turn my back to the world; I remain in your promises in Jesus' name.

2. Father, help me to understand your plans for my life.

3. My youth and mind are renewed to become aware of the precious promises that you have granted unto me in Jesus' name. Amen.

KEY 2
PERSEVERANCE

"Not only so, but we also glory in our sufferings, because we know that suffering produces perseverance; - perseverance, character; and character, hope" (Romans 5:3-4 NIV).

Perseverance means a continued effort to do or achieve something despite difficulties, failure, or opposition; the action or condition or an instance of <u>persevering</u>; steadfastness. It can also be defined as having a determined continuation in something with a steady and continued action of a belief that occurs over a long period of time especially under challenging circumstances.

According to the Bible verse above, we are supposed to rejoice in our sufferings. We can rejoice in them if we know that we are secure in the Lord and with the knowledge that our suffering produces endurance. There will be times when nothing will seem to be working; you may look around, and all you see is darkness, but please remember that you will receive the crown of life at the end of it all. It is through perseverance that character is produced or shaped. Character is important because it distinguishes you from other people. God allows us to go through suffering to produce perseverance, which in turn produces godly character.

2 Peter 1:5-7 says, "*For this very reason, make every effort to add to your faith goodness; and to goodness, knowledge; - and to knowledge, self-control; and to self- control, perseverance; and to perseverance, godliness; - and to godliness, mutual affection; and to mutual affection, love.*" This implies that we not only will have to endure trials of various kinds, but we must count it all joy. The one who perseveres knows that the testing of their faith produces steadfastness. If we desire to live godly lives in Christ, we will suffer persecution. However, the faithful will persevere, and be kept by the power of the Holy Spirit, who is the guarantee of our salvation and who will keep us strong to the end. Perseverance is needed for personal growth. "*Blessed is the one who perseveres under trial because, having stood the test, that person will receive the crown of life that the Lord has promised to those who love him.*" (James 1:12).

James also implores us to persevere under trials because those who do will not only be blessed but will also receive the crown of life that God has promised. Just as the true believer will be eternally secure in his salvation, his faith will also persevere in affliction, sickness, persecution, and the other trials of life that befall all believers. Perseverance reminds you that you have been equipped your entire life for what you are currently facing.

Persevering Christians take prayers seriously as a way of life. They recognize the way of love and forgiveness because they understand the nature of human weakness and seek divine help. They know they had experienced grace beyond their human ability when they gave their lives to Christ. Persevering Christians recognize that the warnings of the Bible are meant for them to obey and that Christ gave His life to change theirs. Therefore, perseverance is a call to faithfulness. It is also a belief that somehow, God will bring His committed people through the difficulties and concerns of life to their promised destiny in Christ despite our failures.

Key Application

1. Take prayer seriously.
2. Recognize the way of love and forgiveness.
3. Obey the commandments of God.
4. Be faithful to God.
5. Have faith in God.
6. Serve others without expectations.

Key Prayer

1. Lord help me to pray, help my prayer life.

2. Help me to forgive during times of temptation.

3. Father, help me to keep your commandments and have your words in my heart. Amen.

KEY 3
EXPECTANCY

"In the morning, LORD, you hear my voice; in the morning I lay my requests before you and wait expectantly." (Psalm 5:3).

Expectancy is a state of expecting or looking forward to a future event with some reasons to believe the event will eventually happen. Having an attitude of expectancy means we should have faith in God's plan, just like Joseph.

We need expectancy in our Christian lives. When we pray, we have an expectancy that God will answer, and we know Jesus responds to faith. Expectations quicken our steps and brighten our eyes as we reach out to future dreams.

"But those who hope [wait] in the LORD will renew their strength. They will soar on wings like eagles; they will run and not grow weary; they will walk and not be faint." (Isaiah 40:31)

The secret to waiting is expectancy. When you believe God will do what He says, you will not give up waiting for His perfect timing. The world's time limits are not God's time limits. Don't stop waiting for God to answer. We can wait patiently when we expect God to be true to His word.

With great expectancy, comes great faith. Faith unlocks the door for God to come. Expectancy opens your heart and enables you to hear and receive from the Lord those things your heart so desires.

> "Do not let your heart envy sinners, but always be zealous for the fear of the Lord. – There is surely a future hope for you, and your hope will not be cut off. – Listen, my son, and be wise, and set your heart on the right path." (Proverbs 23:17-19)

The man who knows and lives out the necessity of expectancy is a man who gets prepared for his work, stays steadfast to his calling, and in due season reaps a bountiful harvest for his diligent labor. Whatever you expect the Lord to do, hold onto it and keep pressing on until you receive it. Don't let go of what you expect just because you didn't get it right then or didn't get it the way you thought you should have.

As a pregnant mother, you must be prepared and highly expectant of the big thing the Lord is preparing for you. Like Mary, the mother of Jesus, you would say, "be it to me according to the word of the Lord". (Luke 1:38)

Key Application

1. Pray and ask God to help you.

2. Read the Bible every day.

3. Replace the negative thoughts with a scripture.

Key Prayer

1. Lord, manifestations of my expectation shall not be cut short, in Jesus Name.

2. Father, let me raise my expectations so they may meet up with your standards.

3. Lord, even though things may not look how I want them to in the natural, I believe that you have a beautiful future and reward for me.

4. May my feet ever walk in your path.

KEY 4

DETERMINATION

"Wait for the Lord; be strong, and let your heart take courage; wait for the Lord." (Psalm 27:14).

Determination is the ability to make difficult decisions and accomplish God's goals based on the truths of God's Word, regardless of the resistance that may be encountered. Determination is also the strength that carries you through the path of success amid obstacles. It is the ability to set ourselves toward Godly pursuits, and not allow ourselves to be distracted or discouraged.

"Who shall separate us from the love of Christ? Shall tribulation, or distress, or persecution, or famine, or nakedness, or danger, or sword? As it is written, "For your sake we are being killed all the day long; we are regarded as sheep to be slaughtered." No, in all these things we are more than conquerors through him who loved us. For I am sure that neither death nor life, nor angels nor rulers, nor things present nor things to come, nor powers, nor height nor depth, nor anything else in all creation, will be able to separate us from the love of God in Christ Jesus our Lord." (Romans 8:35-39)

It takes determination to be an overcomer. By virtue of the fact that you're of God, you will overcome every opposition and challenge in your life. There is nothing that can stand between you and God because the greater One is in you. In the beginning, it may seem like you are losing ground but don't give up, God is on your side.

> "Do you not know that in a race all the runners run, but only one gets the prize? Run in such a way as to get the prize. - Everyone who competes in the games goes into strict training; they don't do it to get a crown that will not last, but they do it to get a crown that will last forever. Therefore, I do not run like someone running aimlessly; I do not fight like a boxer beating the air. – No, I strike a blow to my body and make it my slave so that after I have preached to others, I will not be disqualified for the prize." (1 Corinthians 9:27-27)

Righteous determination requires our persistence to overcome barriers that hold us back--those that can be overcome by more effort, right thinking, clear goals, and help from others. Obstacles that are wrong, misplaced, or laden with sin are the ones to hurdle first. We are to honor obstacles and the timing that God gives, and not rush through with matters for which we are not called or are not ready. Our study of His Word, our prayer lives, and listening to good, godly advice will be our keys to unlocking the right doors and making sure we do not open the wrong ones. Our determination needs to be governed by righteous desire, commitment, and dedication to God's principles. You are on the right track if you have the desire to transform laziness or wrong direction into ways you can improve with sound, biblical, quality goals. If we are driven by pride or just the motivation to excel at all costs, it is a good bet we are on the wrong track and not in this godly character--just into ourselves.

Determination has to do with courage, being strong, and good cheer. God spoke to Joshua several times and in all those times, He kept telling him to be of good courage and be strong (Joshua 1:6-7).

Key Application

1. Determination is essential for success.

2. You need determination to overcome the resistance from your flesh.

Key Prayer

1. Lord, I receive grace to be determined until I become who you want me to be.

2. Lord, grant me the internal fortification to stay with you even when things are not the way they should be.

KEY 5
PRAYER

"Do not be anxious about anything, but in everything by prayer and supplication with thanksgiving let your requests be made known to God." (Philippians 4:6)

Prayer is a means of interacting with God. It is an act, not merely an attitude. We pray to enjoy His presence and tell Him what is going on in our lives. We pray to make requests, **seek guidance**, and ask for wisdom. Fellowship with God is the heart of prayer.

Jesus frequently awoke early to pray. The Bible mentions this in Mark 1:35, *"Now in the morning, having risen a long while before daylight, He went out and departed to a solitary place; and there He prayed."* Therefore, prayer is a massive part of our Christian walk.

"Call to me and I will answer you and will tell you great and hidden things that you have not known." (Jeremiah 33:3)

Prayer clears human obstacles out of the way for God to work. It is not that God can't work without our prayers, but that He has established prayer as part of His plan for accomplishing His will in this world. Prayer gives us direct access to God's listening ear, as well as His love, strength, wisdom, and comfort. It's a way to express our love, confess our sins, and bring our requests to Him.

"Ask and it will be given to you; seek and you will find; knock and the door will be opened to you." (Matthew 7:7). Prayer helps us to participate in God's blessings and provision for us. As we ask for God's help, seek His guidance, and knock on the doors He provides. God's responses draw us closer and involve us in His mighty work.

Prayer is a communion; it is the means of communicating with God. Prayer brings us to align with the plan and purpose of God. It is a means of engaging in spiritual transactions with our faith as currency. When you pray, you must position your heart to receive answers to your prayer. Prayer changes the one who prays, and it is one of the most important keys to unlocking our destinies. The scriptures recorded men who unlocked their greatness through prayer. Our Savior Jesus Christ, Elijah, Paul, and Silas are examples of such men who prayed and got results. When Jesus prayed, He was strengthened to enter the next phase of fulfilling His destiny, which is dying for humanity. Without prayer, He almost wished the cup passed

Him by, but the strength to carry on came upon Him after praying. Sometimes, passion won't be enough; you will need to be driven by prayer. With prayer, you can unlock endless possibilities, become a better person, and even become aligned to the will of God.

Key application

1. Learn to appreciate God through prayer.

2. Pray without ceasing.

3. Pray the word.

4. Be intentional about seeking God through prayer.

5. Pray about everything; there is nothing you can't talk to God about.

Key Prayer

1. Lord help me to pray; give me the grace to pray.

2. Anytime I open my mouth to pray, Holy Spirit, help me not to pray amiss.

3. Give a heart of thanksgiving.

KEY 6
FAVOR OF GOD

"Let the favor of the Lord our God be upon us and establish the work of our hands upon us; yes, establish the work of our hands!" (Psalm 90:17)

God's favor entails God giving us the ability to do something humanly impossible for us to do. The Bible says, *"Surely, LORD, you bless the righteous; you surround them with your favor as with a shield."* (Psalm 5:12). God is willing to bless the righteous and protect them with favor. When the favor of God is upon a man, he will be secured and protected against all oppositions. God shows favor by connecting with His people and being a shield that leads and protects them.

When David found favor with God, (one who was despised by his relatives and was, never presented for Samuel to elect to be king), he became a celebrated person. When you find favor with God, whatever you touch begins to prosper, and people will begin to start to wonder how it happened.

To benefit in God's favor, there are certain things you must do. You must receive God's favor like every other spiritual promise by faith. This was precisely what Mary, the mother of Jesus, did when the angel told her God's plan. In her reply, she said, Let it be unto me according to your word." That is receiving God's favor through faith!

Abraham, the father of faith, did the same. The circumstances looked hopeless when God promised him, that he would be the father of many nations. Looking at his age and Sarah's lifelong barrenness, one would think how could that be possible? They received God's favor and promise by faith. Receiving God's favor by faith is a simple act on our part. And how do you do that? By studying God's Word. Put the Word into your heart and speak it out of your mouth. Then, believe and act on it.

Noah found favor; he was blameless, righteous, and faithful. Joseph found favor with God, as did Esther. God's favor is for a purpose. When He favors you, it's not for you to sit upon, but to do something with. You receive blessings so that you can be a blessing!

Key application

1. Walk with God.

2. Obey God

3. Desire to do God's will.

4. Seek God's wisdom

5. Study the word of God.

Key Prayer

1. Lord, let it be unto me according to your word.

2. Father, increase the desire to do your will in me.

3. I am highly favored in Jesus' name. Wherever I find myself I carry and obtain the favor of God and men. Amen

KEY 7

MEDITATION

> "Keep this Book of the Law always on your lips;
> meditate on it day and night, so that you may be
> careful to do everything written in it. Then you
> will be prosperous and successful." (Joshua 1:7 NIV)

Meditation is the act of filling one's mind with Scripture and dwelling on God and all that He offers to humanity. Meditation involves the whole process of reading and observing a portion of the Scripture in order to seek both its meaning and application. Meditation is designed to motivate and inspire us for the works God has called us to do here on earth.

After Moses died, the Lord gave instructions to Joshua. One such instruction was to meditate on the "Book of the Law," which is also the Bible. Meditating on God's Word should be done frequently, and the actual purpose should be to enrich your understanding so you can apply it to your life.

Meditation is allowing God's Word to control your thoughts. This is important because "...as a man thinketh in his heart, so is he..." (Proverbs

23:7). The way you think has the most powerful influences on the way you live.

Meditation helps to focus your attention on what God has revealed. Furthermore, it helps to calm our souls in God's presence. The prophet Isaiah pointed to the benefit of focused trust in God when he wrote: "*You will keep in perfect peace those whose minds are steadfast, because they trust in you*" (Isaiah 26:3). One of the wonderful benefits of meditation is a greater experience of God's peace in this troubled world.

Meditating helps us overcome sin and the temptation to sin. Psalm 119:11 says that this is so, "*thy Word I have hidden in my heart, that I may not sin against thee.*" Meditating helps us pray biblically. If you spend time dwelling on God's Word, you will find yourself praying over those very Scriptures. Praying through Bible passages strengthens your prayers, keeps your mind engaged and full of faith.

Meditating helps us grow in our knowledge of the Scriptures and of the Lord Himself. The Scriptures reveal God to us; the Word describes His character and His ways; the Bible retraces His steps and helps us trust Him as we walk toward heaven. Taking time to meditate in the spiritual realm makes it a lot easier for God to speak to you and the Holy Spirit to minister to you. You will certainly get refreshed.

Key application

1. Start and end your day with the Word.

2. Talk about God's word.

3. Ask God to open your heart to the truth and wisdom lying within His Word.

4. Apply the words to your own life.

5. Pray the word.

Key prayer

1. I long for your presence, Lord. Lord, quiet my heart and still my soul as I wait on you during these moments alone.

2. I ask you to speak through your Word and in these quiet moments.

KEY 8
WORSHIP

"God is spirit, and those who worship him must worship in spirit and truth." (John 4:24 ESV)

Just as seen by many, worship is not the slow song that we sing. Worship means to acknowledge and ascribe worth to someone or something. Also, worship is declaring the greatness of someone or something. To worship in spirit is to be led by God and know the joy from fellowship with the Holy Spirit. To worship is to delightfully follow God's orders, do what He says, and not thread in the sin that enslaves us. We might love Jesus, but if we don't do what He commands, we can't say that we love Him. It's merely lip-service. When we choose to worship God, we are acknowledging we are not in control. It is a conscious decision to submit to God.

Worship is based on our salvation and reflects the Spirit and truth of God and His Word. Worship reminds us of our position before God and His position above us. The act of worship can be just about anything that honors God. As the Apostle Paul says in Romans 12:1 (NIV), *"Therefore, I urge* you, brothers and sisters, in view of God's mercy, to offer your bodies as a living sacrifice, holy and pleasing to God—this is your true and proper worship."

As we learn more about God through the study of His Word, our hearts will be drawn to worship Him because He is worthy. And, as we worship Him, we will enter a deeper relationship with Him. As we walk with Him, we will learn to trust and love Him. Real worship is not about the songs you are singing, but about your spirit connecting to every word that comes out of your mouth. When you understand who God is, when you see His wonder and greatness, the awesomeness of His splendor, and the beauty of His holiness, then worship will occur.

True worship is based on the desire to honor God. It is offering oneself to God as a vessel to be used for His glory. It requires a personal revelation of God as found in the Scriptures and focusing solely on Him.

When you take your focus away from yourself, away from the circumstances around you, and place it on God in worship, your worry is replaced with trust and acceptance. Worship helps us to align our thoughts with God so that when we make petitions and offer up thanks, we can be assured that we are praying according to His will. God refreshes us when we turn to Him and worship. Even though our circumstances don't change, we will continually be strengthened by Him.

Key Application

1. Create time for worship. Ensure to put away distractions when doing this.

2. Make worship a lifestyle, not just a routine.

Key prayer

1. Lord, give me the grace to worship You to your pleasing.

2. Teach me to understand this mystery called worship.

KEY 9

OBEDIENCE

"... *Behold, to obey is better than sacrifice, and to heed than the fat of rams.*" (1 Samuel 15:22 NKJV)

Obedience is compliance with an order, request, law, or submission to another's authority. Obedience is an important trait one should inculcate in homes, workplaces, and in the communities in which we live.

The Bible asked us to obey the law of Christ, which is the law of love according to John 13:34 which says. "A *new command I give you: Love one another. As I have loved you, so you must love one another*". When you keep God's word, God's word will surely keep you. When you follow God's leading and words in all things, it strengthens your soul because you have a clean conscience, emotional and spiritual strength, and **the ability to meet all of life's demands with certainty.**

When we obey God, we show our trust and faith in Him. Obedience is a daily thing for us to do. Where there is no obedience, there is no trust and no love. If someone claims, "*I know God,*" *but doesn't obey God's commandments, that person is a liar and is not living in the truth. But those who obey God's word truly show how completely they love him. That is how we know we are living in him. Those who say they live in God should live their lives as Jesus did.* (1 John 2:3–6, NLT)

You cannot trust someone without a faithful and sincere relationship. It is impossible to obey someone you do not believe. To love God, you need to know him, and to know Him, you need to spend time with Him, share secrets with Him, ask him for advice, and learn His opinion.

Obedience is the acceptance of the authority and will of God. It includes submitting totally to God and subsequently expressing that submission in actions, words, and thoughts. To be obedient is to agree with God.

Key application

1. Pay attention to God's instructions to you.

2. Write down the instructions in your book.

3. Take steps on them and mark them as done when you've acted on them.

Key prayer

1. Lord, grant me the grace to obey your instructions.

2. Even when doing your word is difficult, help me to always see the need to obey.

KEY 10

FRUIT OF THE SPIRIT

"But the fruit of the Spirit is love, joy, peace, patience, kindness, goodness, faithfulness, gentleness, and self-control. Against such things there is no law." (Galatians 5:22-23)

You must have heard the phrase – "The fruit of the Spirit." But do you know what it means? Before we examine the nine attributes – love, joy, peace, patience, kindness, goodness, faithfulness, gentleness, and self-control, let us get to understand the fruit of the spirit.

Do you know that the expressions of the fruit of the Spirit does not in any way shows that they are different? It is a nine-fold fruit – a unified whole, not operating independently but collectively. It denotes the characteristics of a believer who truly walks in the Holy Spirit. In essence, the fruit of the Spirit is the life of Christ. It is the ultimate life that Christ wants all His children to possess.

The fruit of the Spirit are those traits and characteristics that we begin to see in a man that shows that he has the life of Christ. Matthew 7 from verses 16 to 20 talks about how a good tree is meant to produce good fruits and how you can tell the type of person a man is by the fruit he produces. You can identify people by the fruit they bear. Fruit is an outward expression of the nature of a tree. Some trees have similar leaves but cannot bear the same fruit.

Since we are part of Christ's family, the seed of righteousness has been planted in us. We need to allow such seed to germinate and bring forth the fruit of the spirit. You are what you bear! Have you tried checking the type of fruit that you produce? Have you considered your character and attitudes with respect to the fruit of the Spirit?

You did not choose me, but I chose you and appointed you that you should go and bear fruit and that your fruit should abide, so that whatever you ask the Father in my name, he may give it to you. (John 15:16 ESV).

What fruit is the Bible talking about here? Yes, it is the fruit of the Spirit. There is no doubt about the glorious destiny that God has for us. He has plans and has called us to do great things in glory, but you cannot fully be what God wants from you if you do not bear the fruit of the Spirit.

The verse continues by saying that when we bear fruit, whatever we ask the Father in Christ's name, He will give to us. Bearing the fruit of the

Spirit unlocks your divine destiny and gives you access to ask God the Father for whatever you want.

Key application

1. Take a moment to reflect on the traits and characters that you exhibit.

2. Ask yourself sincerely if you are walking in the spirit. You cannot unlock your destiny if these fruit are lacking in your life.

3. Live a conscious life! Be conscious about the life you live, the way you act and respond to situations.

4. Whenever you see that you are lacking in some aspects, ask God for help.

5. Apart from being conscious, you also must ask the Holy Spirit to guide you and help you.

Key prayer

1. Lord, let the Holy Spirit begin His work in my life so that my life will start to show fruit.

2. Jesus, I want to fulfill my destiny, help me to live a life that is fully conscious to bear fruit.

KEY 11
PATIENCE

> "But those who hope in the Lord, he will renew their strength. They will soar on wings like eagles; they will run and not grow weary; they will walk and not faint." (Isaiah 40:31)

Do you know that while fulfilling our predestined purpose and life calling as Christians, we are faced with uneven circumstances that may tend to spark weariness into the soul of a man? These circumstances and hard times, which are majorly temporal (even when it's long-term), pose a huge challenge to us, calling for endurance, tolerance, and perseverance. These attributes that must be imbibed during this phase can be coined into one word – Patience. It is the capacity to remain calm in the heat of frustration, life's hardships, and adversities.

The mandate of God for every man which can be best termed as "**destiny**" requires persistence to function in the totality of what we have been called into without wavering. Patience is a virtue of the spirit and it is synonymous with forbearance or endurance. From another perspective, patience is a skill that must be acquired if you want to thrive in the world space. It goes alongside self-control, humility, and generosity. It is the nature of God who understands the concept of patience and it is part of the dealings of God in destiny. Acts 26:18 – *"Get up and stand to your feet, for I have appeared to you to reveal your destiny and to commission you as my assistant. You will be a witness to what you have seen and to the things I will reveal whenever I appear to you."* (TPT version).

It helps us to trust and submit to God's plans for our lives as believers until God's desired results are achieved. In fulfilling our life call, there is an expectation of God upon our lives, and we must be able to follow the making processes through to the end to accomplish this mandate as expected of us. God does not expect us to give in to our fears or anxiousness which is a byproduct of the consciousness of "self" but to be patient enough to trust his Lordship in our lives as we sojourn in the path of our destiny. Imitate and follow God closely: The study of the life of God, as well as his only begotten son – Jesus, reveals that patience is a nature of God freely expressed to mankind in excess. Therefore, this nature can be learned from him and he will also grant us the enablement to be patient in our trying times.

Key application

1. Improve by practicing the act of patience always.

2. Meditate often and be mindful of fulfilling purpose even in the heat of life's uneven events.

3. Derive strength in God.

Key prayer

1. Father help me to walk patiently in the manner worthy of what you've called me into.

2. God, I receive the strength to wait upon the spirit to fulfill the mandate for my destiny.

KEY 12

JOY

"These things I have spoken to you, that my joy may be in you, and that your joy may be full"
(John 15:11 ESV)

Have you seen an overjoyed person? Or have you experienced such a feeling? Do you know what it means to have your joy complete? Joy is associated with the mind; you cannot be sad inwardly and say that you are joyful. When you are happy, it comes from within. Joy does not necessarily have to do with what is going on externally; joy happens internally.

Joy is a fruit of the Spirit, and it is not dependent on any external things. Things might be the source of your happiness, but it is a matter of the Spirit of God in you when it comes to joy. You could be going through different challenges and yet still be joyous; that is because joy is not external; it is an internal feeling. I look happy and that is because there is something in me that keeps giving me joy even in a difficult situation.

Jesus spoke in John 15 verse 11 that He wants His joy to be in us so that our joy may be full. If Jesus could say that, then it means that joy resides in us. So, even though the temporary things you see around might give you joy, they cannot provide you with complete joy. Only Jesus can make your joy complete; His type of joy is not temporary, and when He puts His joy inside you, you become overjoyed that even if anything happens around you, you will not be moved because you have the joy of the Lord inside you.

Your joy is not tied to materials things or circumstances. Although things around you might not make you happy, you can choose joy. Joy is so enormously powerful that it can become your strength. *The joy of the Lord is your strength* (Nehemiah 8:10 NKJV). Now that you understand that your strength is tied to your joy, it simply means your joy can empower you on the path to your destiny.

When a man is so much filled with the joy that Jesus has given him; his different challenges do not need to weigh him down again. He receives joy to be able to press on in his life. Even if your future or your destiny seems unknown; and it is like you are burdened with a heavy load, when God sees you are filled with joy, He blesses you abundantly.

Always allow the Holy Spirit to give you reasons to be joyful. Do not focus on your present challenges because it might not allow you to look past your present predicament. Choose to express joy, and when God sees that you are joyous, He takes you to your next position in life.

Key application

1. Find reasons to be joyful. Look around you; do not base your joy on material things or things that cannot give you eternal joy. Let the joy of Christ overflow inside you.

2. Count your blessings in Christ, and you will have reasons to be joyful.

3. When you focus on good and positive things, you will attract better and positive things.

4. Do not be too caught up in the present that you forget the reasons you must be happy. Let nothing stop you from being happy.

Key prayer

1. Lord Jesus fill me with your joy.

2. Lord, let me not bother about my present challenges; help me take my mind off them.

KEY 13

PEACE

"You keep him in perfect peace whose mind is stayed on you because he trusts in you"
(Isaiah 26:3ESV).

Have you ever been in a state of distress or turmoil? What happens when you are in such a state? Does anything else appeal to you? All you would ever want to do now is escape whatever it is that you are going through. Also, at that moment you lose your peace. At such a time, the word 'peace' seems alien to you and you do not even know what it means to have peace. Some people are constantly on the run; running away from something or someone that is haunting them. They do not have peace; they have lost their peace.

It is almost impossible to be on earth without anything that will cause you unrest. There will always be something that tends to make you lose your peace immediately. Peace is a fruit of the Spirit, and any man that is controlled by the Holy Spirit does not suffer from unrest; instead, the Spirit of God fills him with peace. Wherever the Spirit of God is, it does not cause or bring confusion, unrest, or distress; instead, it is calm and peaceful. Peace is not the absence of trouble, but the state of rest that God is in control even though there is a storm on the outside. It is a state of absolute trust in God's promises, protection, and power.

The Bible says in John 16: 33: "*I have said these things to you, that in me you may have peace, in this world, you will have tribulations but take heart, for I have overcome the world.*" That was Jesus speaking there! He says that if you are in this world, distress is unavoidable. He says there is no peace in this world; all you get from this world are tribulations, things that will constantly put you on edge, and things that will come to upset you, but you should be of good cheer because you can still have peace. You can have peace in Him because He keeps in perfect peace those whose minds are stayed on Him. Therefore, you must keep your mind on Christ.

The Bible says, "*Do not be anxious about anything but in everything by prayer and supplication with thanksgiving let your requests be made known to God.*" (Philippians 4:6). Your requests can be made known to God instead of unnecessarily worrying about them. When you are anxious, you lose your peace and begin to worry. No amount of worry will change anything.

Peace doesn't mean you don't have problems; it simply means you have someone you can entrust them with. Worry cannot assure you of a better future, it cannot give you a better way out. Instead, it does more harm to your mind and body. So, stop worrying about how your future is going to be, or what it is all about. Make your requests known to God; that way God sends His Holy Spirit to fill your heart with calmness. When your heart is calm, you will begin to see the plans that God has for you. Things will begin to fall in place, and you will certainly reach your divine position.

Key Application

1. Take note of the things that make you lose your peace; those things that are bothering you, and take them to the Lord in prayer.

2. Disassociate yourself with things that try to cause you unnecessary worry and unrest.

3. Support and fill your heart with God's word so you will not be moved by whatever may want to cause you unrest.

Key prayer

1. God, take away all the things causing unrest in my life.

2. Fill me with your peace Lord Jesus, and cause anxiety and worry to be gone in my life.

KEY 14

LOVE

"So *now faith, hope, and love abide, these three;*
but the greatest of these is love"
(1 Corinthians 13:13ESV).

Love is a word we hear almost everywhere today. Many people use this word, and most times without even meaning it. Love, if not the most popular, is one of the popular fruit of the Spirit. Also, it is the most misunderstood. People perceive or understand love from a carnal point of view.

Love is the greatest virtue a person can have; it is the greatest of all other fruit of the Spirit and it is encompassing. 1 Corinthians chapter 13 is a chapter dedicated to speaking about love. There are a lot of things that are written that talk about love. Love is not angry; it is not boastful.

Love has many more characteristics that we do not know, so we cannot fully grasp the full meaning of Love. Love cannot be defined; it is not a mere emotional feeling or sensation. Love is a person; God is love. True love will flow in and through us when we understand that we are called by love to love. We are to love God and our fellow humans. If love is given a chance, it can redefine or transform everything.

When the Bible says that God is Love, it means that we cannot love unless we ask Him to teach us how to love. There is no love without Christ. Let us check out what God did for us. He created humans, but humans went astray. They acted on their own and neglected God, their creator. This should have made God so angry to destroy the whole human race; instead, He gave His only begotten son to die for the world's sin so that we might not perish. Is there a greater love than this? God has loved us and is expecting us to do the same. He loves us so we can show people how much He loves us.

Love is the greatest commandment God has given to us, and if you are not obeying the commandment that He has given to us (which is fulfilling the mind of God), you will not make God happy. Part of your assignment in destiny is to love. We are called to love. We are not just going to love those who love us, even bad people have people they love. We are to love everyone regardless. You unlock your destiny when you understand that love is a calling. When you show love to people around you, let them feel God's love through you. You must love even if that person is against you;

love even those people who are planning your downfall. Love even when it does not make sense for you to do so. Check this out:

> "You're familiar with the old written law, 'Love your friend,' and its unwritten companion, 'Hate your enemy.' I'm challenging that. I'm telling you to love your enemies. Let them bring out the best in you, not the worst. When someone gives you a hard time, respond with the energies of prayer, for then you are working out of your true selves, your God-created selves. This is what God does. He gives his best—the sun to warm and the rain to nourish—to everyone, regardless: the good and bad, the nice and nasty. If all you do is love the lovable, do you expect a bonus? Anybody can do that. If you simply say hello to those who greet you, do you expect a medal? Any run-of-the-mill sinner does that. "In a word, what I'm saying is, Grow up. You're kingdom subjects. Now live like it. Live out your God-created identity. Live generously and graciously toward others, the way God lives toward you." (Matthew 5:43

Remember, you were once an enemy of God; you also did stuff that God did not like, yet He gave you a chance. He did not kill you but kept you for your glorious future. Show love to the people around you and let them feel what God also did to you. Doing so, brings you a step closer to your destiny. The love you give comes back to you. When you love genuinely, it brings you into alignment with God's nature which is love. When you align with God's nature, then you can align with His plan for your life.

Key Application

1. You cannot love without asking God for help.

2. Ask God daily for the grace to love the people around you.

3. Remember the people who have hurt you even though it seems like they do not deserve your love. Keep praying for them so you can love them enough.

4. Tell more people about the love of God. Whenever anyone offends you, remember that you have a destiny to fulfill, which will not come to pass if you harbor resentment towards the person. So, quickly forgive the person and choose to love.

Key prayer

1. Father Lord, teach me to love. Help me to love as you want me to.

2. Jesus, let me not forget to love even when it seems impossible for me to love others.

KEY 15
SELF CONTROL

> "For this very reason, make every effort to supplement your faith with virtue, and virtue with knowledge, and knowledge with self-control, and self-control with steadfastness, and steadfastness with godliness, and godliness with brotherly affection, and brotherly affection with love".
> (2 Peter 1: 5 – 7 ESV).

What happens when you are having fun? Do you ever want that moment to stop? I do not think so! Most of the time when we are having fun, we do not usually want it to end. They say time flies when you are having fun. That is because we lose track of time when we are having those good moments. It is usually hard to tell yourself – it is enough when you know you must stop. Knowing when to stop and stopping is self-control and we need to exercise self-control in all aspects and areas of life. God is not a man who acts without control; He does not lose His guard.

Do you know that there are many times the Bible mentioned that we should be on guard and be watchful? That is because God always wants us to be in control of our bodies; in control of ourselves. He does not want us to act recklessly or to be loose because the devil can decide to come in when we lose our guard. We must be on guard on so many things; we must be able to control what we say, what we eat, what we do, and a lot of other things. We cannot keep acting any way we like.

1 Thessalonians 4:4 –... *that each one of you know how to control your body in holiness and honor.* That is why we must be in control, so we can be pure and, not lose our guard and allow sin to creep into our lives. We must endeavor not to get carried away with the things of the world.

The devil is constantly on the lookout, watching and looking for loopholes so that he can attack us from such a spot. You should deal with those spots which you do not have control over. You must work on those you are always having problems controlling so that you do not give the enemy a right over your life.

"*Every athlete exercises self-control in all things. They do it to receive a perishable wreath, but we an imperishable*". (1 Corinthians 9: 25 ESV). Do you know who athletes are? Do you know that they go through different phases of training just to keep fit? Some athletes do not eat certain foods, some do not take certain drinks, and that is because they have a goal and a pursuit. You know you have a destiny; you are aware that you have a goal that you are running towards. Do you also know that you need self-control before you can unlock your destiny? You must know when it is okay for you to stop doing what you are doing. You must act like someone who has a purpose and a destiny and not like an ordinary person. You must keep your body under full check and see to it that you do not act recklessly. A loose person cannot be a person of destiny. It must be a self-controlled person.

Key application

1. Identify the things in your life that you still have no control over. Is it your appetite? Your quest for money? Pleasure? Identify and list them out.

2. Begin to work on and pray about the list.

3. As you see that you are overcoming them, you can now begin to cross them off.

Key prayer

1. Father, give me the grace to put my body under control.

2. Anywhere that the devil is trying to attack me because of my lack of self-control, deliver me, Lord.

KEY 16

GENTLENESS

"And the Lord's servant must not be quarrelsome but kind to everyo2Zne, able to teach, patiently enduring evil, correcting his opponents with gentleness. God may perhaps grant them repentance leading to a knowledge of the truth" (2 Timothy 2: 24 – 25 ESV).

How can a person be gentle? What are the traits that are seen in a gentle person? When a man is gentle, he is tender; he is soft, he is not hard-hearted nor strong- headed. A gentle person is not rude, he does not give excuses, and he is not proud. These are traits seen in anyone who is gentle. These days, some people do not want to be called gentle, instead, they want to be associated with violence. They want to become known as hard-hearted. They do not want to be soft. It is so rare to find someone who is gentle, and gentleness is a fruit of a spirit. You cannot claim to be of Christ if you do not have this fruit called gentleness.

Do you know how people pluck fruit from a tree? At times, stones are thrown at the tree so that the fruit can drop. Other times, you might see little children climbing on the tree to shake its branches so the fruit can drop. Whenever stones were being thrown at the tree, or shaken vigorously, did it stop dropping its fruit? No! Do you know you can also be likened to the tree that people want to eat the fruit of gentleness from? When stones are being thrown at you by different people around you, or you are being shaken by different situations you are not to flare up. Show the fruit of gentleness so people can be amazed and your life can be an influence on their lives.

Jesus says in **Matthew 11 verse 29**: *"Take my yoke upon you and learn from me for I am gentle and lowly in heart and you will find rest for your souls"*. Jesus wants you to learn gentleness from Him. Jesus is not harsh, He is not hard-hearted, and He wants you to learn from His life, from His experiences. So, read about Jesus in the Bible, and see how He handled everything and everyone with gentleness and love. There is no better life to learn from than the life of Jesus.

One of the reasons why you need to be gentle is so you can become teachable. A gentle person is not someone who is haughty and so he becomes like a teachable child. You must be like Jesus who is lowly in heart, gentle, and still fulfilled His destiny on earth. You need to learn from Jesus' life in order to unlock your destiny.

Key application

1. Make a conscious effort to continually read and study the life of Jesus.

2. Learn from how He reacts to things and apply them to whatever is going on around you.

Key prayer

1. I want to be like you Jesus; give me the grace to be like you.

2. God, please take away the spirit of stubbornness and hostility in my life.

KEY 17

FAITHFULNESS

"Let not steadfast love and faithfulness forsake you; bind them around your neck; write them on the tablet of your heart. So you will find favor and good success in the sight of God and man" (Proverbs 3: 3 – 4 ESV).

Faithfulness can be said to mean loyalty or to be reliable. When a man marries a woman, it is expected that the man remains faithful to his wife. There should be no other women involved. It takes commitment and loyalty to stay faithful. Faithfulness is for an exceptionally long time. Some people are faithful to a particular brand that they buy; they cannot switch or change the brand. That is exactly how faithfulness should be. It is a point where no matter what happens, you cannot change. It takes ages and time to break some people's loyalty. For some people, it even takes death to break it. If you decide to stay faithful, you cannot do it and later stop. Faithfulness requires consistency.

Now, if a man is unfaithful to his wife, do you think that such a man can maintain faithfulness with God? What are the things that show unfaithfulness towards God? When a man is unfaithful towards God, he shares the time that he is meant to spend with God on other things. He shares his heart that is meant to be God's abode with other things. A man becomes unfaithful towards God when he is more faithful to other things. Just imagine a scenario where you cannot afford to miss that TV show at 8 pm but can go the whole day without reading your Bible in the morning. You know we do some things, and we think that they do not matter but they do matter to God. God expects a relationship with us, and a relationship cannot last if one party is not faithful to the other party.

Now the Bible says that God is faithful but who can find a faithful man? We all profess that we love God, but are we faithful in our relationship with Him? Do we not have other things that we share the love of God with?

"One who is faithful in a very little is also faithful in much, and one who is dishonest in a very little is also dishonest in much. If then you have not been faithful in the unrighteous wealth, who will entrust to you the true riches? And if you have not been faithful in that which is another's, who will give you that which is your own? (Luke 16: 10 – 12)

Another way we do not realize our unfaithfulness is when we cannot see the things God has placed us to be in charge of. God has a destiny for us; He has our future planned for us, yet we misuse it. We act unfaithfully. Just like how a master leaves the house help in the charge of the house when he is not around, that is the same way that God has placed some things in our care right now. How faithful are you to it? Some forget about God and just act recklessly. When you do so, you are unfaithful to the man that has kept you in charge of just a little thing. How do you now want to receive what belongs to you? Some things that God gives to us are to test who we are going to be when He places us with what is ours. We don't always know this, so we become unfaithful. Your faithfulness towards the little things will prove how God will release greater things to your hands (Luke 19:17).

Key application

1. Realize what God has placed you in charge of and be faithful.

2. See to it that you are faithful in your relationship with God. Let nothing make you unfaithful towards God.

3. Set time apart for God so you can have a healthy relationship with Him.

Key prayer

1. God, cleanse all the ways that I have been unfaithful towards you.

2. Help me to be able to be faithful in the little that I have been put in charge of.

KEY 18
GOODNESS

"For we are his workmanship, created in Christ Jesus for good works, which God prepared beforehand, that we should walk in them" (Ephesians 2:10 ESV).

We say that God is good all the time, and all the time, God is good. It is an extremely popular saying. People try to associate goodness with God, and they feel like it is only God that can be good. When there is a miracle, we exclaim and say God is good! We seem to have forgotten that goodness is a fruit of the Spirit which means that God expects us to be bearing such fruit to people around us.

We should bear in mind that God created us, and since He has goodness embedded in Him, he created us for good works; for goodness. There are a lot of good things that God wants us to do. He wants goodness from us. You are in Christ to show forth the goodness of your Father in heaven.

What are these good works that God has created us to do? Let us use the life of Dorcas as an example. Dorcas was a woman who was full of good works and doing good to all the widows that were around her. When she died, those widows mourned her and sent for the disciples to come and attend to her. What could have made those widows cry? They mourned her because her existence had been doing something for them. She must have been giving them warm clothes; or perhaps, she gave them food. She was involved in good works and proved to be impactful in their lives.

What kind of life are you living now? Are you good to the people around you? Are you living a life that can impact the people around you? Have people seen the good works in you?

Psalm 119 verses 68: *"you are good, and you are the source of good; train me in your goodness"* (MSG). You cannot be good without God the source of goodness, who does all things well. You need God to help you bring out the goodness that he has kept inside of you.

The kind of life that you live, can affect your destiny. Is your life full of good works? Do things to help; let your life show forth the goodness of God, and your record of good works will determine if your destiny shall be attained. Are you living a life worthy of emulation, or are you living as you please? Just as your heavenly Father is good, and nothing He does is bad, you should also live in that manner. You should come into this life to make an impact with the good works that God has embedded in you. Show your good works to all men so they can see the glory of the Father in you. That way, you will be able to be closer to your destiny.

Key application

1. Since God has kept goodness inside of you, begin to list out a few good works that you can do for the people around you, the society you are in, and make effort to start doing them.

2. Do not ever get tired of doing good things because that is a way to impact people's lives around you.

3. Never stop praying to God to help you to be do and good.

Key prayer

1. Father forgive me for the different ways that I have refused to show good works (Goodness).

2. God, teach me how to be good to everyone around me.

KEY 19

KINDNESS

> "Be kind to one another, tenderhearted, forgiving
> one another, as God in Christ forgave you"
> (Ephesians 4:32 ESV)

Kindness is having a benevolent, friendly, generous, warm-hearted nature to others. All these attributes are part of kindness. A kind person is friendly and generous. Such a person is approachable and will let people in when they come to them with matters that bother them.

A kind person doesn't like to see people suffer. It breaks their heart to watch people suffering and they will look for ways to relieve their pain. Now, I am telling you that a lot of people in the world today are not even bothered about the pain of their neighbors, friends, or even families. Even if you do not have the means to help those people, their condition should move you to tears, and you should pray for them. But what do we do? Most times, we just act nonchalantly to people who are in need. Jesus was a compassionate man; He was kind. His heart broke when he saw the need of the people. The Bible said, "And Jesus had compassion on them." How many people have you had compassion on? How many people have you been kind to?

If people need help around you, help them because they need to be shown love and compassion. Show them the spirit of kindness that God has placed inside of you.

The merciful, kind, and generous man benefits himself (for his deeds return to bless him), but he who is cruel and callous (to the wants of others) brings on himself retribution (Proverbs 11:15 AMP).

This is a great blessing to those who are kind. If you are kind, you have nothing to lose, because your deeds return to bless you. Those little acts of kindness will not go unnoticed before God because He sees them. Let them be he reason why He will bless you in return. When you are kind, apart from helping others, you are doing yourself a favor and keeping blessings for yourself in the future.

Your life should be a solution to people who need help. Anyone who fulfills their destiny did not get there without being kind to people. There are people that the person helped who will later be a source of blessing in the future.

People are also the stepping stones that God will use to place you at the point of your destiny and at times, God has strategically placed those people around you so you must be of help to them first. We are sometimes blind to that fact; we think that everyone who needs our help is all about money, so we refuse to help. Help is not limited to money alone; it could be in the form of advice, or even just a short word of prayer for the person, but you still refuse to help. You have only delayed your destiny. You do not know the role the people around you are to play in your destiny. So, if you are kind to them, they can help you get to where you need to be.

Key application

1. Pray to ask God to open your eyes to the need of the people around you.

2. Do not neglect the needs of people around you especially when you know that you can help.

3. Look for things that you can do to make an impact in your environment/ place of work/ church.

Key prayer

1. God, give me a heart that is kind and compassionate.

2. Help me not to be blind to the needs of the people around me.

KEY 20

THE WORD OF GOD

"Your word is a lamp unto my feet, and a light unto my path." (Psalms 119:105)

The word of God is most times referred to as the Bible. This may not be true as the Bible contains the words of different people and personalities. Such as men from their own understanding, angels, the devil, God, Jesus -- different conversations make up the Bible. However, the word of God is the manifestation of the mind and will of God. It is what the Lord is saying at a particular time concerning a particular issue. The word of God is *".... every word that proceedeth out of the mouth of the Lord"* (Deuteronomy 8:3).

In the beginning, for the destiny of the earth to be revealed or made manifest, the word of the Lord played a major role. In Gen 1:3-27, the creation of everything on earth was by the word of God; "And God said, let there be..." Those statements made by God in that portion of the Bible are what the earth needed for it to enter the state God desired, and has been the source of its sustenance.

Psalm 119:105; "*Your word is a lamp unto my feet, and a light unto my path.*" The word of God leads us, guides us, and serves as a pointer toward the direction we are to take. Furthermore, when we ask God to speak to us, He communicates through diverse means, such as vision, Bible, prophecy, and people, among others. In Gen 15:1 the word of the Lord came to Abram in a vision, to comfort, reassure, and reaffirm His promise to give him an heir from his own flesh and blood. The birth of Jesus and His destiny was prophesied years even before his parents were born. When it was almost time for the prophecy to be fulfilled, an angel came and prophesied. Mary and Joseph accepted the words of God from the mouth of the angel and fulfilled them. Even Jesus knew the words of God concerning his life and lived by them during his lifetime. Isaiah 7:14; Isaiah 9:6: Matthew 1:20-23; Luke 1:28-32.

In the quest to unlock destiny, you need directions, encouragement, and guidance. One cannot unlock a destiny that one does not know, or how do we get a confirmation that the destiny we seek to unlock is really our destiny? Just as the book of Psalms 119:105 said that, the word of God illuminates our path, it tells us what to do, how to do it and when to do it. The word of God encourages -- when we are on the road to fulfilling our destiny, different challenges may come but the word of God comforts and encourages and even proffers solutions. He alone knows why He created us, and how He wants our life played out. Therefore, we must ask Him always so that we will not miss our destiny.

The Lord hears the prayers of his children, Isaiah 59:1 "*.... neither his ear heavy, that it cannot hear us.*" When we pray for directions, he will lead us. Also, when the words of God come to us, through whatever means, it is pertinent that we heed, so that things can unfold as it's meant to according to the will of God. It is not enough that we seek God's voice just to know our destiny but that we keep seeking Him as we go unlocking doors and fulfilling our destiny.

Key application

1. Read and study your Bible daily.

2. Seek to know your destiny by asking God in prayer.

3. Trust Him enough to know that He is too experienced to mess with your life.

Key prayer

1. Lord, direct me to the path I must take to my destiny.

2. When your words come, help me to obey and work with them promptly.

KEY 21

THE SPIRIT OF GOD

"And I will pray the Father, and He will give you another Helper, that He may abide with you forever" (John 14:16 NKJV)

The Spirit of God is His personality. It is the sphere in which God operates. In the Old Testament, it signifies, God's breath (Job 33:4). They spoke of it as His vital power or spirit, which was as active and as efficacious as God Himself. The Spirit of God is divine.

In nature, God is Spirit, John 4:24. After Jesus got baptized at the River Jordan, the Spirit of God descended upon Him as a dove, Matthew 3:16. The Spirit of God that descended on Him marked the beginning of His ministry and drove Him into the wilderness to get Him prepared. The Spirit of God in the scriptures came upon men and expressed itself in different dimensions. The Spirit of God and the word of God work together. In the beginning the Spirit hovered while the word brought everything to existence. At Jesus' baptism, the word declared Him as the Son of

God, while the Spirit bore witness and drove Him into the wilderness to teach and nurture Him.

The Spirit of God is very crucial in the journey of unlocking destiny. Even in the beginning, before the Lord spoke things into existence, the Spirit of the Lord was hovering in the darkness trying to decipher and take into cognizance what needed to be done to bring the earth into destiny (Genesis 1:2). The Spirit of God knows everything because He is always there looking and searching. The Spirit of God is a teacher. When the word of God comes, He helps us to understand and guide us in all truth. He teaches us, guides us, and helps our infirmities. He teaches us when to submit, speak, remain silent, and take caution. The Spirit of God does not just teach or search, He also guides, and helps to dream dreams and see visions (Joel 2:28; Acts 2:17).

The spiritual reproductive process starts with God's Spirit joining with our human spirit: "*The Spirit [itself] bears witness with our spirit that we are children of God, and if children, then heirs— heirs of God and joint heirs with Christ, if indeed we suffer with Him, that we may also be glorified together.*" (Romans 8: 16-17). As joint heirs with Christ, we will receive dominion over all things, even our breakthrough to a fulfilled destiny. The

Holy Spirit knows God's plan for us and guides us to fulfill it.

Key application

1. The Holy Spirit is our Companion and Comforter in our journey to our destiny.

2. You can talk to the Holy Spirit. You can seek His direction always.

Key prayer

1. Lord, today, I ask that you fill me up with your Spirit.

2. Help me to listen and obey the leadings of the Spirit.

KEY 22

THE PLAN OF GOD

"for I know the thoughts I think towards you, saith the Lord, thoughts of peace, and not of evil, to give you an expected end." (Jeremiah 29:11)

The plan of God is the will of God for our lives. Just as every plan is drafted towards an end, so is the plan of God, to bring an expected end. God is a God of order; He does things precept upon precept (Isaiah 28:10). A person may have many ideas concerning God's plan for his life, but only the designs of his purpose will succeed in the end (Proverbs 19:21). The Lord works everything together to accomplish His purpose (Psalm 33:1).

As humans, there is always a desire to make things work and make plans towards it, but we often make plans without putting God's plan into consideration. This attitude does not in any way affect the efficacy and authenticity of God's plan for us. Furthermore, the role of God's plan in our lives cannot be downplayed, which is why before making decisions, we must seek to know His plan..

The plan of the Lord is communicated to a man by the word of God, through diverse means. God said in Jeremiah 29:11, "*For I know the thoughts I think towards you, saith the Lord, thoughts of peace, and not of evil, to give you an expected end.*" Of course, the plan of the Lord would seek to bring, glory, joy, happiness, comfort, provision, among others; it does not seek to bring pain or anguish. God revealed His plans to make Joseph head over his brethren to him in a dream. Although, the process did not seem like it, he was mistreated by his brothers (Genesis 37:27; Genesis 39:1). It appeared his destiny was truncated, but in the end, his destiny was fulfilled. David in the Bible was also mistreated; people sought after the death of his destiny, for he had been anointed to be the next king of Israel, even before the reigning king died. Even King Saul, the first king to rule over Israel, tried to kill him, because he was envious of the hand and power of God in his life, but the will of the Lord still came to pass.

Whenever God makes promises, we should be assured that He will bring them to fulfillment. God declared in Isaiah 55:8-9, that our ways are not His and our thoughts are not His thoughts. We might have made plans for ourselves, but only the plans of God can lead and bring our destiny to fulfillment because He created us and knew us even before we were born (John 1:6; Jeremiah 1:5).

The plan of God is the map that shows direction and helps build our strength.

God respects us so much that He does not come in or come along except we invite Him. He is not like one of those rude people we know. Therefore, to know His plans, we have to invite Him first and build a relationship with Him, then He can start revealing His plans for us. However, when there is no trust, we may lose faith in His words and may miss the end, or its fulfillment might be delayed.

If you want to fulfill your God-given destiny, you will need to make wise choices all along the way. Whether you seek direction on where to go to school, which job to take, who to marry, or where to live, nothing is more important than knowing God's will. The Bible says, *"Trust in the Lord with all your heart, and lean not on your own understanding; in all your ways acknowledge Him, and He shall direct your paths"* (Proverbs 3:5-6). It is a promise!

Key application

1. Seek to know God's plan.

2. Write the things God is revealing to you about your destiny.

Key prayer

1. Father Lord, please reveal your plans for my life.

2. Help me to trust your plans for my life Lord.

KEY 23

RIGHTEOUSNESS

> *"Thou hast loved righteousness, and hated iniquity; therefore God, even thy God, hath anointed thee with the oil of gladness above thy fellows."* (Hebrews 1: 9)

Righteousness is an attribute that belongs to God and is manifested in His laws. No man can be justified by his own works apart from God's ordinance. Righteousness is the quality of being right in the eyes of God. It is, therefore, based upon God's standard because he is the ultimate law- giver.

Hebrews 1: 9; *"Thou hast loved righteousness, and hated iniquity; therefore God, even thy God, hath anointed thee with the oil of gladness above thy fellows."* We are joint- heirs with Jesus Christ (Romans 8:17). He has been anointed with the oil of gladness and has been raised above us, because of His righteousness. According to the prophecy in the book of Isaiah 61:3, the oil of gladness is meant to replace mourning and sorrows. He received it because He loved righteousness and hated iniquity; He did not support iniquity at all.

Reuben, Jacob's first born, was supposed to enjoy some benefits as the first born, like: getting a double inheritance, (he and his father's). However, because he committed the iniquity of laying with his father's concubine (Genesis 35:22), he lost his inheritance as the firstborn. His birthright was not shared among his brethren but among the children of his brother Joseph's sons, - Ephraim and Manasseh. The kingdom was given to Judah, and the priesthood to Levi. His brothers excelled above him, for sin brought him down. The consequences of this act of unrighteousness did not only affect him; it also affected his tribe. No judge, prophet, ruler, or prince came from his tribe, except for Dathan and Abiram who were noted for their rebellion against Moses.

The Oil of Gladness is given so that man may celebrate and be comforted, without any reason to mourn. Even when there may seem to be a delay, or when there are reasons to quit, it comforts us. All unrighteousness is sin, and the sinful nature is not pleasing before the Lord. It is only a man that is righteous that can commune with God, and only a man that communes with God can hear the voice of God. We must bear in mind that we will get to know the plans of God for our lives when He speaks with us. Also, we must discern that He will not speak where there is no relationship. For righteousness exalts a nation, but sin is a reproach to any nation. Righteousness makes one worthy of any upliftment, direction, and leading from God.

God is righteous and Christ is the only righteous person other than God. Christ did not become righteous by prayers, but by obedience. Therefore, for a man to be righteous he must obey God and be willing to do all His commandments.

Key application

1. Love righteousness and righteous living

2. Hate iniquity and things the Lord hates.

Key prayer

1. Father Lord, teach me your ways so I may be righteous in your sight.

2. Lord, help me to live righteously and godly in this present world.

KEY 24

THE POWER OF WISDOM

> *"Wisdom is the principal thing; therefore get wisdom. And in all your getting, get understanding."* (Proverbs 4:7 NKJV)

Wisdom is the ability to discern what is right from what is wrong. It is a gift that gives us the capacity to make the right choice(s) or decision(s). If knowledge is power, then wisdom is using the power the right way. There is wisdom from people and wisdom from God. God's wisdom can make one wise man more powerful than ten rulers (Ecclesiastes 7: 19).

Rebekah, the mother of Esau and Jacob, loved Jacob more and wanted him to have the blessings of their father Isaac (Genesis 25:27). This blessing was originally meant for his brother Esau, who was the oldest. Jacob, however, applied wisdom with determination to take the blessings from Esau at all cost. Rebekah tricked her husband Isaac, and in the long run, changed the destiny of her children (Genesis 27: 8-29). David's destiny to become king over Israel may not have come to pass if he had not known when to flee. When

King Saul sought to kill him, David fled and hid till it came his time to rule (1 Samuel 19:11-12). And when David had the opportunity to kill Saul, he did not because he recognized and respected the anointing of God on Saul.

On the way to fulfill our destiny, we meet different people, and they may be instrumental in our breakthrough, or they may be destiny helpers. A single tree does not make a forest, according to a popular proverb. Wisdom will help a man follow peace, even with enemies. When we are people of wisdom, then we can relate with people without difficulty. Then we can give respect to who it is due, get excused when necessary, contribute when we ought to, know when and what kinds of offers to accept or decline, what circle of friends to keep, and the list goes on. The ability to relate well with people is the power and strength received from wisdom, which makes our journey smooth. Wisdom is also needed to discern between spirits, when the voice of the Lord comes, we will be able to recognize it and distinguish it from every other voice, just like John in Revelation.

Relying on the words of Jesus in Matthew 7:7, there is an assurance that when we ask, God will do whatever we ask for. Therefore, in order to live out your destiny, admit that you lack wisdom, then ask God for wisdom; James 1: 5.

Key application

1. Learn God's wisdom by learning from scriptures.

2. Memorize a verse each day from the book of Proverbs.

Key prayer

1. Fill me with your wisdom Lord, in all my dealings.

2. Help me to utilize your wisdom for my success.

KEY 25

FOLLOWING JESUS

"Then He said to them, "Follow Me, and I will make you fishers of men." (Matthew 4:19 NKJV)

Jesus is the way, the truth, and the life: no man cometh unto the Father, but by Me. John 14:6. Following Jesus does not entail going to church alone, it is only part of what it entails. In fact, one can be a church goer and not encounter the power of Jesus. There are different kinds of people who go to church (Mark 1:23). Following Jesus means that we submit under Him totally. We might have had plans on how we want to live our lives. But when we come to acknowledge the plan of God, we should know that God's plan is bigger than our plan. More so, our life is no longer ours (Galatian 2:20). It is no longer what we like to do, but what He tells us. We follow Jesus by surrendering our will, desires, and plans.

Jesus in Matthew 4:19 told Simon Peter and Andrew his brother, "Follow me and I'll make you fishers of men." These men before they met Jesus were fishermen, passionate and diligent towards their work. In fact, Jesus intervened in their matter when He saw they had toiled all day without results. However, as beautiful and merit-deserving as their efforts were, that was not the plan God had for them. The call from Jesus marked the beginning of their journey unto destiny. And all the years they spent with Jesus was to prepare them for their own Journey. He taught them in the ways of the Lord. He fed them with the words of life that they may grow. He showed them the path to go. While they were with Him, they lacked nothing and were satisfied.

John 1:1; "*In the beginning was the Word, and the Word was with God, and the Word was God.*" This verse makes us realize that Jesus has been there from the inception and knows everything about us even before we were born (Jeremiah 1:5). The fact that he became flesh and dwelt among us, John 1:14, means he understands our plight. He knows how being a human can be, little wonder he solicits for us to be in the presence of the Father: 1 John 2:1, 1 Timothy 2:5. Walking with Jesus while on the journey to unlocking your destiny is the best thing to do, because there is an assurance that there is one that understands and is strong enough to help with arms wide open. Following Jesus will align us with purpose.

We must drop our will, and in turn trust, and obey. We must cast all our cares on Him and not worry about how things will play out (Matthew 6: 34; Proverbs 4:25). Just like a little child trusts you to catch him/her whenever you throw him/her in the air; this is the same way He wants you to follow him on any path He leads you. Finally, we must deny self. Mark 8: 34, *"And when he had called the people unto him with his disciples also, whosoever will come after me, let him deny himself, and take up his cross, and follow me."* When we can do these things, then he will lead us to the path to our destiny, and he will help us through the doors as we go.

Key application

1. Be resolute about following Christ.

2. Put Christ first always.

Key prayer

1. Help me, Lord, to drop my will, so that I may follow you diligently on the path you would take me.

2. Lord Jesus, I invite you to take the lead while I follow.

KEY 26

FRIENDSHIP

> *"All this is done by God, who through Christ changed us from enemies into his friends and gave us the task of making others his friends too."*
> (2Corinthians 5:18)

The role of our relationships in our sojourn in this world in one way or the other affects the fulfillment of our life's call. Friendship is one of the forms of relationship, and it is building a mutual affection between two or more people. It builds a stronger form of interpersonal bond that is liable to influence our individual lives and decisions. It is a long-lasting period of combining affection, loyalty, love, respect, and trust. It is important to note that the interest of the people involved in this bond can affect our day-to-day functionality, either positively or negatively. Therefore, the element – 'friendship' is an especially important factor that should be intensely considered before such decisions are made.

As Christians, Jesus is our model in building the right and meaningful friendship that would encourage us to be on track with God's call for our lives and destiny. God also showed us the true concept of friendship through Jesus. 2 Corinthians 5:18 – *"All this is done by God, who through Christ changed us from enemies into his friends and gave us the task of making others his friends too."*

One of the greatest commandments that Christ came to establish is that we love one another just as He has loved us. However, it is necessary to spend more time investing in friendships that draw us closer to God and always infuses us with the consciousness of purpose rather than otherwise. This statement was also established in 2 Corinthians 6:14 – *"Do not try to work together as equals with unbelievers, for it cannot be done. How can right and wrong be partners? How can light and darkness live together?".*

It is not a jinx that the right friendship helps to increase you and helps an in-depth self-discovery. Meaningful friendship enriches our vision of God's mandate for mankind. It perceives the value of man as an existing entity on earth and helps to keep a man aligned to the greatness of God that has been imputed in us. It helps us to locate our power level, dimensions of authority, and unlock our potentials. Fulfilling our life's mission becomes easier when we have people we trust and love, people who help us to fast-track the discovery process in God. A biblical friendship that reflects Christ in action is termed a covenant friendship. This is a form of friendship that is not bounded by love alone but is also rooted in destiny and purpose. There is a heightened level of loyalty in this friendship and God is also placed first. It is propelled by the power of the spirit and it becomes stronger when the parties involved fix their gaze on God who first showed man the greatest form of steadfast love.

Key application:

1. Choose your friends wisely.
2. Flee from ungodly friends.

Key prayer:

1. Dear Lord, connect me with meaningful individuals who will help me walk in the path of your purpose for my life.
2. God, strengthen my relationship with my divine and destiny friends.
3. Dear Lord, help me to cut bonds with those I am presently entangled with who would lead me astray.

KEY 27
DILIGENCE

"And beside this, giving all diligence, add to your faith virtue and virtue knowledge" (2 Peter 1:5)

Have you ever wondered why it is important to be devoted to what you do in achieving the purpose of God for your life? Diligence entails paying rapt attention to a task and giving the required care to a particular situation. Diligence is one of the virtues that God mandates for a man showing how important this element is to the fulfillment of God's purpose. It is a heavenly gift that can be coveted and transferred into an individual. The energy we exert into what we do determines the progress rate of such a particular task and how fast the desired success would be achieved. It is a skill that can be learned and instilled into our daily lives and activities. Besides, in destiny, there is an expected time frame assigned to the specific task given by God to a man in our sojourn in heeding to the call of God for our lives.

God keeps a record of our progress in destiny instead of the assigned time frame for each of His divine tasks assigned to us. Concerning this, we can establish that diligence is a virtue that must be imbibed if we want to walk according to God's plan for our lives. 2 Peter 1:5 "*And beside this, giving all diligence, add to your faith virtue and virtue knowledge*". Progress in our divine assignment can only be achieved when we put the needed care, attention, persistence, focus, and determination to the vision and mandate that has been given to us by God. This reveals to us the yardsticks of God in defining the success of a man.

God measures our success based on how well we have been able to fulfill His desired course for our lives and not based on our physical possessions, wealth, or material things. Since it is God's wish for His creatures to be successful, fruitful, and gain dominion on earth (our first assignment), He then instructs us as Christians to exhibit this priceless virtue termed "**diligence**" always in what we do or engage in per time.

The role of diligence in accessing the possibilities of life and in the unraveling of the depth of destiny fulfillment cannot be over-emphasized. Diligence comes with a lot of rewards such as blessings, wealth, excellence, promotion, etc. A biblical example of a man who was very diligent in fulfilling his course on earth is Jacob. (Gen 31:38-41)

The bedrock of diligence is determination and discipline. It is best developed by making a conscious decision to make it a habit.

Key application

1. Rely on God for life's productivity.

2. Avoid procrastination.

3. Be disciplined.

Key prayer

1. God, empower me to be diligent and persistent in the fulfillment of your call upon my life.

2. I receive the grace to be dedicated to my divine assignment.

KEY 28

KNOWLEDGE

"My people perish because of lack of knowledge"
(Hosea 4:6)

It is interesting to know that being endowed with the capacity to reason is a byproduct of a man's psychological result of perception, learning, and reasoning. The mind and mental state of a man must be tuned to the consciousness of gaining knowledge daily before there can be an increase in the capacity of a man, and a shift in the present state of a man.

To start with, we must define the keyword in today's devotional, which is knowledge. Knowledge is the practical or theoretical understanding of a defined subject. It is further defined as what is consciously or unconsciously learned, understood, and aware of. It is of a common saying that "Knowledge is power," and this statement shows that the intensity of a man's dominance is determined by how much and how well he has accumulated knowledge in the space of time either by experience or any other means.

God is so keen about men seeking and growing in knowledge. In Hosea 4:6, God said; *"My people perish because of lack of knowledge."* Over the years, ignorance has been one of the powerful tools utilized by the devil to truncate the destinies of men who God called to live, take dominion, and multiply on the earth which He created. As a believer, you must inhale the light that comes from knowledge often to stay ahead in fulfilling God's purpose for your existence. It is quite easy to deviate from the plan of God and His customized calling for your life when the element of knowledge is missing. Knowledge keeps us equipped with the necessities of destiny accomplishment that brings the greatest glory to God and achieves maximum expansion of God's kingdom.

A believer who is deficient in knowledge needs to seek and acquire the knowledge required to fulfill purpose according to the radar of God's creation for man. There are basic channels to seeking knowledge rightly, but the first step is to build an intimacy with God who is the giver of knowledge in abundance. This can be built through intense and continuous fellowship with the father. Fellowship comes in the studying of the word and tarrying in prayer. However, reading, setting goals, doing research, and so on are also ways by which knowledge can be acquired.

Conclusively, we have established that seeking knowledge always keeps you on track in the fulfillment of God's purpose for your creation. God is interested in how well we can daily seek to learn and yearn for the establishment of His kingdom on earth by walking according to the path He has designed for us individually.

Key application

1. Build intimacy with God.

2. Seek knowledge always.

Key prayer

1. God, overshadow me with the spirit of knowledge and the light of my purpose.

2. Father, supply me with all the necessities needed to walk according to the precepts of my creation.

3. Even as I seek to know and learn daily, Father empower me with the grace to continually seek and stretch me to the maximum capacity needed to fulfill my destiny.

KEY 29

HOPE

"Who against hope believed in hope, that he might become the father of many nations, according to that which was spoken, So shall thy seed be."
(Romans 4:18 KJV)

There are different definitions to hope. Hope means believing that good things will happen when we have faith in God. Hope can be directed inward in faith or outward in expectations. Hope helps you look forward to a better you, better days, better circumstances, and better things. Hope can empower your vision to look beyond your present situation and see the beautiful destiny awaits you.

Without hope, it will be difficult to have faith. Hope keeps us alive, living, and fighting for the better. Without hope for the better, many would have given up. One of the most important possessions in life is hope. In the above verse, Abraham had unwavering hope. When it seemed everything about him having a child pointed in the opposite, he still had hope due to his faith in God.

Sometimes, I wonder how Abraham did it. He did it because he had hope, and not just faith.

Faith makes God grant the request we make; hope prepares us to receive it. With hope, there are endless possibilities, even if it seems there is no way forward. When it looks as if you want to give up your quest to discover and fulfill your destiny, hope keeps you going.

The Bible says: *"Now hope does not disappoint, because the love of God has been poured out in our hearts by the Holy Spirit who was given to us"* (Romans 5:5 NKJV). Can you see that? Hope does not disappoint. People can disappoint you; things can disappoint you or even you can become disappointed in yourself, however, hope does not disappoint. So, whenever it seems like you are experiencing some sort of disappointment, you must use your key of hope to keep going.

There are times in life when we are faced with difficult challenges, and we are pained. However, this can be inevitable; but with hope, you will see beyond the challenges you are currently facing. Hope offers you a lens to see beyond the present. Joseph saw beyond the hatred of his brothers, the ridicule of slavery, and the pain of being a prisoner. Even after his brothers realized he was the prime minister, hope made him reveal to them that while they thought they treated him badly, God meant it for good (Genesis 45). Hope makes you look beyond people's bad treatment towards you, and see God's plan. With hope, you can see God in the midst of your trying times.

Key Application

1. Engage your mind to see who you want to become when you don't even look like it yet.

2. Don't feel bad when you are facing challenges; look beyond the challenges.

3. Let the thought of your future bring a smile to your face.

Key prayers

1. Lord Jesus, help me see beyond the present.

2. God, give me the grace to hope against hope.

KEY 30

FEAR OF GOD

"The fear of the Lord is the beginning of knowledge; fools despise wisdom and instruction."
(Proverbs 1:7)

Over the years, it has been established that having a profound respect for God has a lot to do in defining our purpose as individuals. Having a good understanding that the originator of a man's destiny is God, we can always take a step further with Him while fulfilling the mandate he has given unto us by subjecting ourselves to His directions and decisions. From creation, the fear of God was opened to mankind as the only way a man can be aligned to the purpose of our creation per time. Adam and Eve failed their assignment in the Garden of Eden because the fear of God was undermined. However, our conscious efforts as individuals can't always match up with the yardstick of the fear of God. The fear of God is a spiritual gift. Being God-fearing is a quality that automatically directs the course of our lives positively and affects other aspects of our being by the purpose.

Proverbs 1:7 – "*The fear of the Lord is the beginning of knowledge; fools despise wisdom and instruction.*" The total reverence for God is the path to tread upon to more insight into our divine calling. It reveals to us our genetic codes and the potentials locked up in us. The one who has kept these virtues in us has the know-how of how we can unlock the life that He has preprogrammed for us. Our true and original personality is illuminated when we continually subject ourselves to God (the fear of God).

Our primary function is that we replicate God here on earth. "*...ye are gods*" (Psalm 82:6). This explains that there is a part of God's DNA in us and that's why we can replicate His person here on earth. However, we can only become like the one we fix our gaze on. We can reveal out of place if we don't shift our focus from His pace, which is another form of reverencing God as the director of our lives. The fear of God is first a consciousness then a requirement. It is a deliberate longing to live in sync with God's moral standard and to honor him even as we learn at his feet. The goodness of life, purpose, discovery, and blessings of God are tied to the depth of reverence we have for God.

"But we all, with open face beholding as in a glass the glory of the Lord, are changed into the same image from glory to glory, even as by the Spirit of God." (2 Corinthians 3:18)

Key application

1. Be disciplined to commit yourself to the ordinances of God.

2. Meditate on God's word daily, learn from those who had a deep reverence for God in the scriptures, and continually embrace God's correction.

Key prayer

1. Father, I receive the fullness of your revelation.

2. Dear Lord, heighten my obedience, true servanthood, and give me the grace to honor and reverence your words even as I replicate you here on earth.

www.ingramcontent.com/pod-product-compliance
Lightning Source LLC
Chambersburg PA
CBHW071619040426
42452CB00009B/1391